SPOTTER'S GUIDE TO
HORSES
& PONIES

Joanna Spector

Illustrated by David Wright,
Elaine Keenan and
Malcolm McGregor

SCHOLASTIC INC.
New York Toronto London Auckland Sydney
Mexico City New Delhi Hong Kong Buenos Aires

Edited by Alastair Smith, Felicity Mansfield and Tim Dowley
Designed by Karen Tomlins and Joanne Kirkby
Series designer: Laura Fearn
Cover designer: Adam Constantine
Additional illustrations: Andy Martin and Ed Roberts
Expert consultant: Juliet Mander

The original publisher would like to thank the following individuals
and organizations for photographs:
Cover — © Jerry Irwin/Science Photo Library; pp. 1, 2-3, 10-11 — © Kit
Houghton Photography/CORBIS; pp. 4-5 — © W. Perry Conway/CORBIS;
pp. 6-7 © Peter Johnson/CORBIS; p. 7 (mr) © Digital Vision;
pp. 12-13 — © Annie Griffiths Belt/CORBIS; pp. 14-15, p. 18, p. 19 — © Kit
Houghton Photography; pp. 16-17 — © Buddy Mays/CORBIS.

ISBN 0-439-40764-8

CONTENTS

4 How to use this book
6 The story of horses
7 Using horses
8 Looking at horses
9 Colours and markings
10 Points of the horse
12 Horse and pony care
13 Stabling
14 Feeding
16 Grooming
17 Shoeing
18 Riding
19 Tack
20 Ponies
32 Riding horses
46 Harness horses
53 Draught horses
60 Web sites
61 Useful words
62 Scorecard
64 Index

HOW TO USE THIS BOOK

This book is a guide to identifying horse and pony breeds from all over the world. The breeds are arranged with ponies first, followed by riding horses, harness horses (bred to pull light carriages) and draught horses (used for pulling heavy loads).

Next to each picture is a short description of the breed, telling you where it originated, what kind of work it was bred for, the colours it can be, and its height.

Some colours and markings have unusual names. You can look them up on page 9. If there are any other words you don't understand, look in the list of useful words on page 61, or check the diagram detailing horse parts on pages 10-11.

These horses live wild on the Great Plains in Wyoming, USA. They are descended from riding horses.

SPOTTING A BREED

When you see a breed, make a tick in the circle next to its description. Some types of horse only live in certain parts of the world, and others are very rare indeed. However, you might spot them in wildlife parks, in movies or on the television.

The chart on pages 62-63 lists every breed shown in this book. Note the date that you see each breed on the chart. You'll build up a record of the breeds that you've spotted.

Name of breed	Date
Dartmoor	8/6
Døle	8/6
Don	5/7
Dutch Draught	10/11

Fill in the chart like this.

5

THE STORY OF HORSES

The first horses were small and deer-like. They lived in woodlands, 50 million years ago. They evolved into swift, sure-footed beasts that were good at escaping from enemies.

All modern breeds of horse are descended from two ancient types, the southern type and the northern type.

Humans are thought to have begun to control and breed horses in Europe, several thousand years ago. Today, there are about 200 different breeds of horses.

The only truly wild breed left in the world is the Przewalski, from the Gobi Desert in Mongolia, where some still live in herds.

These horses' long legs and slender bodies are signs that they are descended from southern-type horses.

The southern type was light and swift, with a silky coat, like a modern Arab horse.

The northern type had a thick, rough coat and sturdy legs, like a modern Exmoor pony.

USING HORSES

Originally, horses were hunted for food. Later, they were bred for specific types of work. For example, some were bred to pull light carts and carriages day after day. Heavier types, meanwhile, were bred for ploughing and pulling heavy carts and wagons.

Today, people ride mostly for pleasure or sport, although some horses still work on farms, especially in poorer countries.

In the 1800s Arab horses, which are small, nimble and swift, were crossed with English hunters, which are strong and hardy, to produce Thoroughbreds. This fast, tall and beautiful breed is now used for racing all over the world.

Racing thoroughbreds

LOOKING AT HORSES

At first, it can be tricky to tell what breed a horse or pony is. Here is a quick guide to certain clues.

A curved-in face (called a dished profile) and a tail held high means that the animal probably has some Arab blood.

A small, sturdy build and a long, rough coat are signs that it is probably a mountain or moorland pony.

A very tall, lightly built horse, with long legs, a fine skin and coat is probably a Thoroughbred.

A big, slow horse with heavy features and feather (long hairs) around its feet is probably a draught horse.

CROSS OR PURE BRED?

Most horses and ponies are cross bred, that is, descended from different types. You are likely to see pure-bred horses and ponies at:
- Horse shows.
- Stud farms, where horses are bred.
- The breed's natural surroundings; for example, hills and moors in Britain, lowlands in France or Belgium, or mountains in Austria.
- Racing stables or racecourses.
- Riding stables.

COLOURS AND MARKINGS

Here are nine of the most common coat colours and patterns, and the proper names for them.

Bay

Chestnut

Black

Grey

Dun

Brown

Strawberry roan

Piebald

Skewbald

FACE MARKINGS

Star

Snip

Stripe

Blaze

LEG MARKINGS

Sock

Stocking

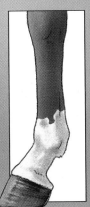
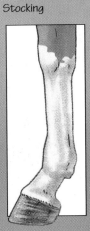

POINTS OF THE HORSE

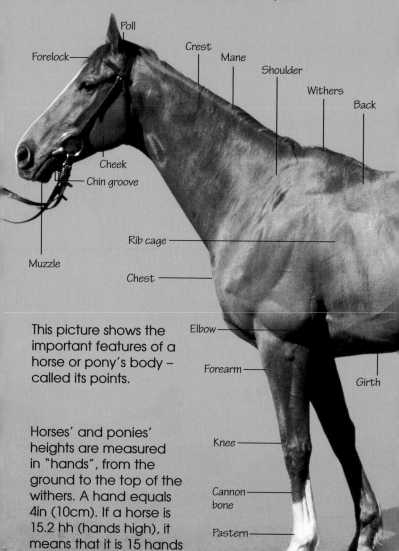

Poll

Forelock—

Crest

Mane

Shoulder

Withers

Back

Cheek

Chin groove

Muzzle

Rib cage —

Chest —

Elbow—

Forearm—

Girth

Knee —

Cannon bone

Pastern—

Forelegs

This picture shows the important features of a horse or pony's body – called its points.

Horses' and ponies' heights are measured in "hands", from the ground to the top of the withers. A hand equals 4in (10cm). If a horse is 15.2 hh (hands high), it means that it is 15 hands and 2 inches high.

HORSE OR PONY?

Whether an animal is called a horse or a pony depends on how tall it is. If it is over 14.2 hands high (hh) then it is classed as a horse. If it is 14.2hh, or less, then it is called a pony.

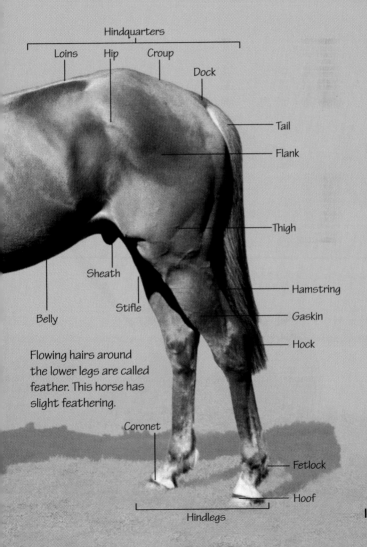

Hindquarters

Loins   Hip   Croup

Dock

Tail

Flank

Thigh

Sheath

Hamstring

Stifle

Gaskin

Belly

Hock

Flowing hairs around the lower legs are called feather. This horse has slight feathering.

Coronet

Fetlock

Hoof

Hindlegs

HORSE AND PONY CARE

Wild horses and ponies live in groups, moving about together. To keep your horse or pony happy, let it live outside, as it would in the wild, as much as you can. To keep it healthy, follow these guidelines.

Ponies enjoy the freedom of outdoor life.

- Let it live in a field with other horses and ponies.
- Allow enough room for grazing. A pony needs at least 4000m² (one acre) to provide it with fresh grass.
- Change fields in spring and autumn if the grass is thinning, to allow the grass to grow back.
- Clear up droppings.
- Provide plenty of fresh drinking water.
- Make sure that there is shelter in the field, such as trees, or a shed.
- Ensure that the field's fencing is strong, to stop escape attempts. Also, make sure that fencing is safe, to prevent injuries.

STABLING

During really cold winter spells, you should keep your animal in a stable. Follow these tips so that it stays happy and healthy.

• Exercise the animal every day. Ride for an hour, or turn it out into the field for a few hours.
• Feed it properly. It needs hay to nibble during the day and night, and high energy food such as corn, in the morning, at night and perhaps at midday.
• Give plenty of fresh water.
• Clean the stable daily. Remove wet bedding and droppings to stop smells and foot disease.

• Put down fresh bedding regularly.
• Groom the horse every day, to keep its coat and skin clean and healthy.
• If your animal is clipped, it will need to wear rugs in winter. Seek advice from an expert, so that you know just how much protection is needed.
• Always let fresh air into the stable to lessen the chances of your animal catching coughs and colds.
• If you want to change your feeding and exercising routines, alter them gradually. Horses and ponies don't like change. They need time to adjust to new ways.

FEEDING

In its natural environment, a horse or pony eats small amounts of bulk food (mostly grass) almost non-stop throughout the day. Those kept in stables eat hay instead of grass. During the summer, horses and ponies are kept outside, and probably need no food other than grass. However, during the winter, they need a supplement of hay.

EXTRA FEEDS

As well as hay or grass, a horse may need high energy or "short" feeds. Use corn or cubes, mixed with another type of food. (Corn is either oats or barley. Cubes are also called nuts.) You should seek advice from an expert about what would suit your animal best, and on how to prepare the food. Different horses have different needs.

Foods you can add to corn or cubes are:
• Bran, but only in small amounts.
• Chaff. This is made of chopped hay.
• Sugar beet, soaked for 24 hours prior to feeding.
• Small amounts of linseed, for a shiny coat.

FEEDING GUIDELINES

How much, and what, you give to your horse or pony will depend on its size, temperament, health, how much exercise it gets, the time of year, and how much good grass is available.

These are the basic rules for feeding:
- Always make sure that it has enough grass or hay to eat.
- Feed a little and often. It will not be able to digest large meals properly.

- Always have fresh drinking water available.
- Wait for at least an hour after feeding before you ride your horse or pony.
- Give feeds at the same time each day.
- If there's no grass, give juicy vegetables or fruits, such as carrots or apples.
- Make sure that you give the animal access to a salt block.

Horses should have access to fresh water, particularly at feeding time.

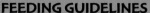

GROOMING

There are lots of grooming tools. Each has a different use. Here's a selection.

- A hoof pick is used for cleaning inside the hooves.

- Dirt and stains are taken off an unclipped coat with a dandy brush, working back from the top of the neck. Always brush in the direction of the coat.

- If the animal is kept in a stable, a body brush can be used to clean the skin and coat. Don't use this brush on a field-kept horse, though – it strips the body oils that keep the animal warm, dry and healthy.

- A sweat scraper removes excess sweat or water from the coat.

- A thin coat of hoof oil is brushed on the hooves to make them shine and stop them from splitting.

- Strapping pads are made of stuffed leather. Use them to groom the neck, shoulders and hind quarters, shortly after exercise. The pad shines the coat, and massages the muscles to tone them.

- A water brush is long and narrow, with short bristles. Used damp with water, for smoothing the mane and tail after brushing.

- Brushes are cleaned by pulling them across a rubber or metal currycomb.

SHOEING

Most working horses and ponies need to wear metal shoes to stop their hooves from getting worn down. Shoes also stop the hoof becoming cracked, bruised or out of shape. Horseshoes must be made to fit properly, by a blacksmith – also called a farrier.

Unless a horse is being rested, new shoes should be fitted every 4-6 weeks. The shoes are nailed to the animal's hooves. It does not hurt, but some animals find the experience a little worrying at first.

PARTS OF THE HOOF

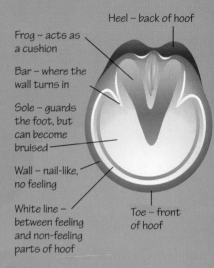

Heel – back of hoof

Frog – acts as a cushion

Bar – where the wall turns in

Sole – guards the foot, but can become bruised

Wall – nail-like, no feeling

White line – between feeling and non-feeling parts of hoof

Toe – front of hoof

PARTS OF A SHOE

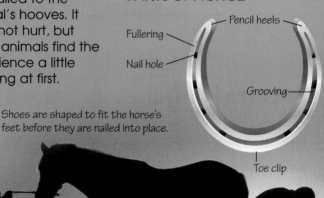

Pencil heels

Fullering

Nail hole

Grooving

Toe clip

Shoes are shaped to fit the horse's feet before they are nailed into place.

RIDING

There are two main styles of riding:
• English style. This developed from an old European style of riding and is now practised all over the world.
• Western style. This grew out of cattle ranching work in North and South America. Mostly it is used in the Americas for rodeo displays, modern ranch work and long-distance trail riding.

Riders of either style learn to sit so that the horse is well balanced and can move freely. They learn to control a horse using a combination of their hands, legs, body and voice.

If you would like to learn to ride, find a riding school that is approved by a horse society (details on page 60), so you can be sure that your teacher is qualified.

English-style riding

TACK

ENGLISH SADDLE
Also called a "General Purpose Saddle".

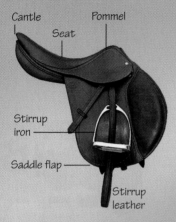

Cantle
Seat
Pommel
Stirrup iron
Saddle flap
Stirrup leather

SNAFFLE BRIDLE
One of several bridles used in English-style riding.

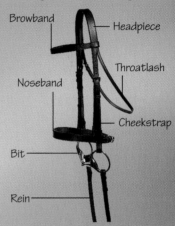

Browband
Headpiece
Throatlash
Noseband
Cheekstrap
Bit
Rein

WESTERN SADDLE

Cantle
Horn
Cheyenne roll
Seat
Fork
Front jockey
Side jockey
Saddle strings
Fender
Wide tread stirrup

WESTERN BRIDLE

Browband
Throatlash
Cheekpiece
Curb strap
Western curb bit
Rein

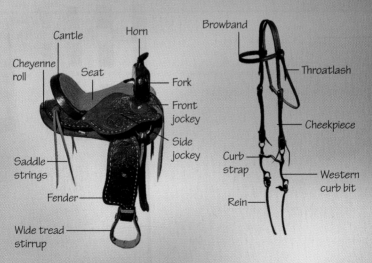

PONIES

⬇ HIGHLAND

Largest British pony. From the Scottish Highlands. Once used as a pack pony, now popular for trekking and driving. Usually grey or dun, can be black or chestnut. Up to 14.2hh.

Long, thick mane

Long, thick tail

Coat is long in winter

Thick, short neck

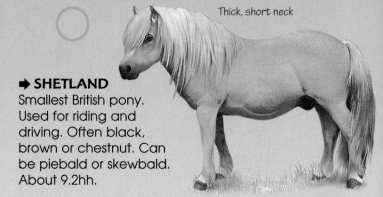

➡ SHETLAND

Smallest British pony. Used for riding and driving. Often black, brown or chestnut. Can be piebald or skewbald. About 9.2hh.

⬇ DALE

From the Pennine hills, northern England.
Used for pony trekking and as a harness
pony. Usually dark brown or
black. May have white
markings. Up to 14.2hh.

Lots of
feather

⬇ FELL

From higher regions of the western
Pennines. Usually black, sometimes
brown or bay. No white
markings. About 14hh.

PONIES

⬇ EXMOOR
Oldest British breed. Lives half wild on Exmoor, south-west England. Hardy. Good riding pony. Bay or brown with light coloured underside. Up to 12.3hh.

Rough, springy coat

Light coloured muzzle

⬇ DARTMOOR
Lives half wild on Dartmoor, south-west England. Hardy and sure-footed. Excellent riding pony. Bay, black or brown. About 12hh.

Small, pretty head

⬇ CONNEMARA
From north-west Ireland. Ancestors probably Spanish and Arab horses. Jumps well. Usually grey, but often dun, black, brown, bay or chestnut. 13-14hh.

Elegant neck

◄ NEW FOREST
From New Forest, southern England. Good riding pony. Size and markings vary, but not piebald or skewbald. Up to 14.2hh.

PONIES

⬇ WELSH MOUNTAIN
Old breed from Wales which has Arab
and Thoroughbred blood. Popular
show pony. Great for children.
Usually grey or chestnut.
Up to 12hh.

Tail
carried
high

Arab-type
head

⬇ WELSH COB
Descended from Welsh ponies
and Andalusian horses. Strong.
Most colours, except piebald
or skewbald. 14-15hh.

Arched
neck

Deep,
strong
body

⬇ HAFLINGER

From the Tyrol mountains, Austria. Strong and sure footed. Ideal for pulling heavy loads on steep hillsides. Good for riding and driving in harness. Chestnut. About 14hh.

Heavy head

Flaxen (yellow) tail and mane

Thin neck

Sloping croup

➡ GOTLAND/RUSS

Originated on island of Gotland, Sweden, in Stone Age. Good trotter and jumper. All colours, often brown, bay or chestnut. About 13hh.

Light build

25

PONIES

⬇ ICELANDIC
Bred from various northern European ponies. Used as riding or pack pony. Quiet and friendly. Any colour; often grey, dun, brown, black or chestnut.
12-13hh.

Lifts knees high when moving

Black and silver mane and tail. Mane grows short and straight, like a crest.

➡ FJORD
Comes from Norway. Good for driving, haulage, carrying and riding. Mostly yellow-dun. 13-14hh.

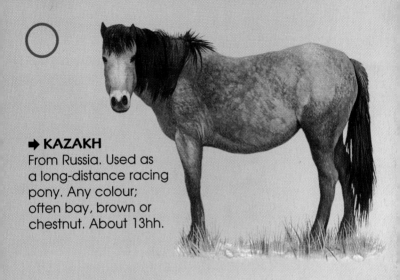

➡ KAZAKH
From Russia. Used as
a long-distance racing
pony. Any colour;
often bay, brown or
chestnut. About 13hh.

⬇ HUÇUL
From the Carpathian mountains of
Russia and Romania. Strong pack pony,
probably related to Tarpan breed.
Brown, dun or bay. About 13hh.

Short
neck

PONIES

⬇ CASPIAN

Wild pony, from Iran. Very few remaining.
Looks like a miniature Thoroughbred. Good
jumper. Usually bay or brown, sometimes
grey. Never has white marking.
9.2-11.2hh.

Long legs

Muscular
hindquarters

➡ CRIOLLO

From South America.
Survives well in
poor conditions.
Dun, roan, brown,
skewbald, black,
or bay. About 14.2hh.

⬇ CAMARGUE

From swampland at mouth of river Rhone, France. Tough and strong, many still live wild. Foals are born brown, but usually become grey. 14.2hh.

Large head

Coarse coat

Long, silky coat

➡ FALABELLA

Miniature horse, from Argentina. Not strong, but used as a driving pony and children's pet. Any colour. Less than 7hh.

PONIES

⬇ PRZEWALSKI

Also called Asiatic or Mongolian
Wild Horse. Only about 300 exist –
either in captivity or in herds on
Gobi Desert, Mongolia. Bay or
dun. 12-14hh.

Upright mane

Thin
tail

Large
head

⬇ TARPAN

Oldest breed in Europe and northern
Asia. Can be seen living wild in Poland.
Usually brown with black ears,
mane, tail and legs.
13hh.

Coarse mane
and coat

⬇ PONY OF THE AMERICAS

New breed, from the USA. Good
riding pony. Spotted. Looks similar
to Appaloosa horse, though
smaller. 11.2-13.2hh.

Dark
muzzle

Rounded body

⬇ SABLE ISLAND PONY

From Nova Scotia, Canada. Small
and tough. Lives in wild herds. Feeds
off scrub grass on sand dunes.
Often chestnut.
About 14hh.

Light
build

RIDING HORSES

⬇ THOROUGHBRED

Bred in England from Arab
horses. World's fastest breed.
Powerful and elegant. Black,
brown, bay, grey or chestnut.
15–16.2hh.

High
withers

Neat
head

Long legs

Dished
profile

Tail carried high

➡ ANGLO-ARAB

Cross between
Thoroughbred
and Arab. Fast,
strong, handsome.
Excellent all-rounder.
Same markings as
Thoroughbred.
About 16hh.

⬇ APPALOOSA

Bred by native North Americans. Good in all uses. Markings vary, though mainly identified by spots and splashes of pink and white. 14-15.3hh.

Pinkish muzzle

➡ AMERICAN SADDLEBRED

First bred as riding and harness horse in southern USA. An excellent riding horse. Bay, brown or chestnut. 15-15.3hh.

High tail

High knee action

33

RIDING HORSES

⬇ MORGAN
Originally bred from one American
stallion named Justin Morgan. Solid,
well-muscled. Bay, brown, black
or chestnut.
14-15.2hh.

Thick tail

Deep, elegant body

⬇ TENNESSEE WALKING HORSE
From USA. Has three unusual gaits:
flat-footed walk; running walk;
running canter. Trots only when
in harness. Solid markings.
15-16hh.

Head
nods with
each step

Long
pasterns

➡ QUARTER HORSE

From USA. Named after quarter-mile races. Quick and intelligent. Any colour. 15-16hh.

Short neck

Sloping croup

➡ PASO FINO

American, descended from Spanish explorers' horses. Does not trot at all. Can be any colour. 13-15.2hh.

RIDING HORSES

⬇ SHAGYA ARAB

Eastern European horse bred from Arabs.
Tireless. Popular as cavalry horse in
World War One. Usually grey.
14-15hh.

Tail carried
high

Small, fine
head with
dished profile

Large eyes

Stong back

➡ POLISH ARAB

Bred in Poland since
1500. Used as general
riding horse and
racehorse. Tough and
strong. Popular in USA
and England. Can be
bay, grey or chestnut.
14.2-15.1hh.

Straight profile

Thick, arched neck

➡ ANDALUSIAN

From Southern Spain. Ancestors were Barb and Arab, plus native ponies. Good riding horse. Grey, black, bay or brown. 15.2-16hh.

⬇ LUSITANO

Portuguese horse. Same ancestry as Andalusian. Used by army, on farms and in bullrings. Grey, brown or bay. 15-16hh.

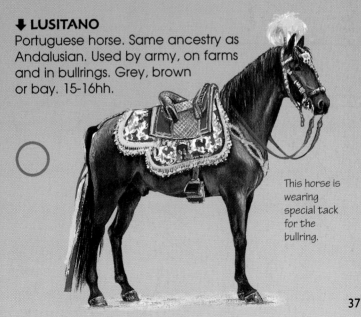

This horse is wearing special tack for the bullring.

RIDING HORSES

⬇ BUDYONNY

From Rostov, in Russia. Can live on poor food. Once used as a cavalry horse. Now often used for long-distance riding and racing. Brown, black, bay or chestnut. About 16hh.

Long neck

Upright shoulders

Strong legs

⬅ DON

Comes from the Don Valley, Russia. Survives well on poor grass. Has lots of stamina. Always chestnut. 15-16hh.

High, narrow body

➡ AKHAL-TEKE
Ancient breed from Turkmenistan. Has many uses. Can stand great heat or cold. Golden chestnut, bay, black or grey. About 15.1hh.

Fine coat with metallic sheen

⬇ KARABAIR
Comes from the mountains of central Asia. Fast and good natured. Can work in dry, hot weather. Equally good for riding or in harness. Grey, bay, black or chestnut. 14.2-15.2hh.

Fine, thin tail

RIDING HORSES

⬇ PALOMINO
Popular in the USA. Descended from Arab horses. The name can refer either to the breed or the colour. Mostly bred as show horses. Any shade of chestnut, with white mane and tail. 14-16hh.

Often has white face markings

Overo marking type

⬅ PINTO
Bred in the USA. There are two marking types: overo and tobiano. Overo is mostly dark, with white patches. Tobiano is mostly white, and has dark patches. Various heights.

➡ TURKOMAN
Comes from
Turkmenistan and
northern Iran.
Strong and tireless.
Good riding horse.
Usually grey or bay;
but also dun or
chestnut. 14.3-15.2hh.

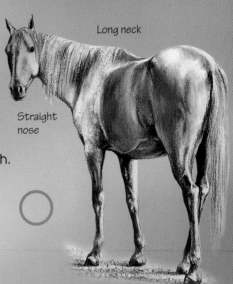

Long neck

Straight
nose

⬇ TRAKEHNER
Bred mainly in Poland and Germany.
Used as a farm and cavalry horse.
Gentle but brave. Very good
sports horse. Bay, brown, black
or chestnut. 16-16.2hh.

Sloping
shoulders

RIDING HORSES

⬇ DØLE/GUDBRANDSAAL

Also called Ostland or Dølehest.
From Norway. Strong, medium size.
Originally used as a pack horse.
Usually black, brown or bay.
About 15hh.

Strong
neck

Lots of
feather

➡ SELLE FRANCAIS

Cross-bred in France
from Anglo-Arab and
other horses. Brave
and strong. Excellent
for riding and sports,
especially jumping.
Often chestnut.
15.2-16.3hh.

↓ HANOVERIAN

German breed descended from war horses ridden in the Middle Ages. Strong. Good sports horse. Any solid colour; often bay or brown. 16-17hh.

Strong hindquarters

Heavy shoulders

➡ HOLSTEIN

German breed. Big and strong. A good carriage and sports horse. Usually brown, bay or black. 16-16.2hh.

43

RIDING HORSES

➡ KNABSTRUP
Danish breed
descended from
a spotted Spanish
mare. Popular as
a circus horse.
Fast and hardy.
Always spotted,
usually white with
black spots.
About 15hh.

*Short,
arched neck*

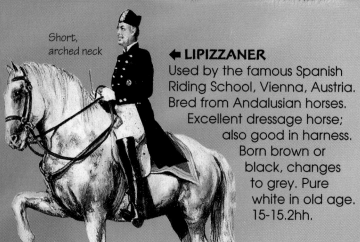

⬅ LIPIZZANER
Used by the famous Spanish
Riding School, Vienna, Austria.
Bred from Andalusian horses.
Excellent dressage horse;
also good in harness.
Born brown or
black, changes
to grey. Pure
white in old age.
15-15.2hh.

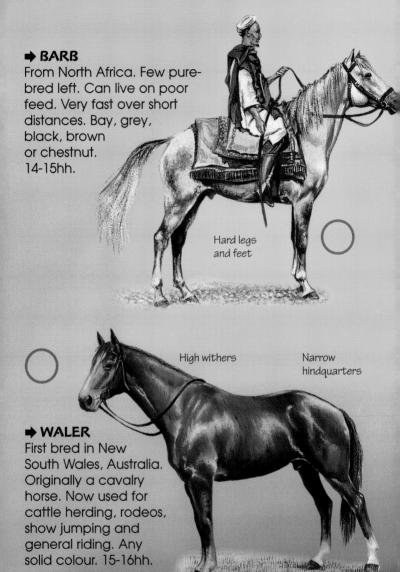

➡ BARB
From North Africa. Few pure-bred left. Can live on poor feed. Very fast over short distances. Bay, grey, black, brown or chestnut. 14-15hh.

Hard legs and feet

High withers

Narrow hindquarters

➡ WALER
First bred in New South Wales, Australia. Originally a cavalry horse. Now used for cattle herding, rodeos, show jumping and general riding. Any solid colour. 15-16hh.

45

HARNESS HORSES

➡ STANDARDBRED

Trotting horse, from the USA. The name comes from the fact that trotting horses had to achieve a certain speed, the "standard", before they were allowed to race. Any solid colour; usually bay, black or brown. 15-16hh.

Long body

Long back

➡ ORLOV TROTTER

From Russia, named after Count Orlov. Strong and fairly heavy. Once used as a cavalry horse. Often grey, also black or bay. 15.2-17hh.

Some feather

Thick, curly mane and tail

➡ FRIESIAN
From Friesland, in the Netherlands. Bred in the Middle Ages to carry knights in armour. Strong and good natured. Always black. About 15hh.

⬇ GELDERLANDER
From Gelderland, in Netherlands. Once worked on farms. Now used for riding and harness work. Chestnut, grey, bay or brown. 15.2-16hh.

Tail carried high

Wide body

HARNESS HORSES

➡ GRONINGEN
Farm horse, from the Netherlands.
Heavy, but fast. Can live on poor food.
Good in harness or for riding. Usually
black, bay or brown. 15.2-16hh.

Deep, strong
body

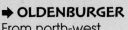

➡ OLDENBURGER
From north-west
Germany. Big, strong,
fairly fast. Popular
carriage horse, used
for riding, too. Usually
grey, bay, black or
brown. 16.2-17.2hh.

Sloping shoulders

➡ CLEVELAND BAY

From Yorkshire, England. Sure footed, not fast. Used for carriage work. A good jumper. Always bay, without white markings. 16-16.2hh.

⬇ HACKNEY

English, high stepping trotter, famous for exaggerated but graceful action. Popular at horse shows, it is often used to pull light carriages. Bay, black or brown. 14.3-15.3hh.

High tail

Long back

HARNESS HORSES

⬇ KUSTANAIR

From Kazakhstan, Central Asia. Three types:
Steppe, Riding and Basic. The Steppe is
heavy and slow, Riding is light, and the
Basic is between the two. Has solid
colours, usually
chestnut or
bay. 15-15.2hh.

This is the lighter,
"Basic" type of
Kustanair.

➡ FINNISH

Mainly used on
farms and in forests
in Finland. Gentle
and tireless. Also
used for trotting races
and riding. Most are
chestnut, often with
white markings.
About 15.2hh.

➡ FREDERIKSBORG

An old breed from
Denmark. Hard
working. Used on farms
and for riding. Srong and
lively. Usually chestnut.
Up to 16hh.

Short legs

⬇ KLADRUBER

From Czech and Slovak regions of Europe.
First bred in sixteenth century, for Emperor
Maximilian II. Often used on farms
and in dressage competitions.
Black or grey. 16-17hh.

Prominent,
curved
nose

HARNESS HORSES

⬇ NONIUS

Hungarian. Named after an Anglo-Norman stallion that founded the breed. Black, bay or brown. Has a large size range – from 14.2-17hh.

Smallish eyes

This is the "Light" type of Wielkopolski

➡ WIELKOPOLSKI

Polish. Many types: heavy ones are used on farms; light ones to drive or ride. Usually bay, brown or chestnut. About 16hh.

DRAUGHT HORSES

➡ CLYDESDALE
Scottish. Strong and
active, but not very
heavy. Popular on
farms. Bay, brown or
black, with white on feet,
face and underside.
About 17hh.

⬇ SHIRE
The classic English draught horse. Once
carried knights in armour. Later used
on farms and to pull heavy loads, such
as beer wagons. Hard worker, usually
bay, black or grey, with
white markings.
Up to 18hh.

Lots of
feather

DRAUGHT HORSES

➡ SUFFOLK PUNCH
From Suffolk, England. Short and stocky. Does well on little or poor food. Very good natured. Always chestnut. About 16-16.2hh.

Thick neck

Wide chest

⬅ IRISH DRAUGHT
Good all-round farm horse, from Ireland. Makes a very good sports horse when crossed with a Thoroughbred. Bay, grey, chestnut or brown. 15.2-17hh.

Silky, dapple
grey coat

➡ PERCHERON
From Northern
France. A popular
working horse.
Very strong. Often
weighs over a ton,
but needs little
food. Good to
work with. Black or
grey. 15.2-17hh.

Heavy neck and
shoulders

◀ ARDENNES
From France and
Belgium. Was used
by Napoleon's
cavalry. Powerful
but gentle. Can live
out in bad weather.
Chestnut, roan
or bay. About
15.2-16hh.

DRAUGHT HORSES

⬇ BRETON HEAVY DRAUGHT
From north-west France. A strong, rugged working horse. Usually strawberry roan in colour, but can be bay or chestnut. 15-16hh.

➡ PINZGAUER NORIKER
The oldest Austrian breed. Quiet and strong. Excellent for pulling ploughs. Bay, chestnut or spotted. 15-16hh.

Short legs

Arched neck

➡ AUXOIS
Ancient French
breed. Once used
for carriage and
farm work. A
powerful working
horse. Usually bay
or strawberry roan.
Never black or
grey. About 15.2hh.

Muscular body

⬅ TRAIT DU NORD
From northern France.
Similar in shape and
temperament to the
Ardennes. Quiet and
gentle. Usually bay,
roan or chestnut.
About 16hh.

DRAUGHT HORSES

➡ AVELIGNESE
Bred mainly in
Tuscany, northern
Italy. Originally
used as a pack
pony or a light
draught horse.
Short and muscular.
Usually chestnut.
About 14.2hh.

Flaxen
(yellow)
mane
and tail

⬅ VLADIMIR
From Vladimir,
Russia. Used for
heavy and light
harness work. Bay,
roan or chestnut.
About 16hh.

Very deep
body

➡ JUTLAND
Danish. Once used by
the Vikings. Mostly used
as a farm horse and
as a brewers' draught
horse. Chestnut, black,
grey, bay or light
brown. 15.2-15.3hh.

Very short
legs

USEFUL WORDS

all rounder – horse or pony that is good at different things, such as hunting and gymkhana games.

cob – short, stocky horse (about 15.3hh). Quiet and well behaved.

colt – male horse up to three years old.

dressage – training of a horse to master basic skills plus more difficult, precision movements.

event horse – used in horse trials, which include dressage, show jumping and cross-country riding.

filly – female horse up to three years old.

flat racing – racing over short course without jumps.

foal – horse or pony up to one year old.

gelding – male horse that has been operated on so that it cannot breed.

gymkhana – show where short races and mounted games are held.

horse – fully grown horse that is over 14.2hh.

hunter – strong horse that can gallop cross-country and jump fences.

hurdler – horse that races and jumps small barriers, called hurdles, usually over courses about 4km (2½ miles) long.

mare – female horse over three years old.

pony – fully grown horse that is under 14.2hh.

school master – old, well-behaved, well-schooled horse or pony. Safe and reliable for people learning to ride.

show horse/pony – competes at horse shows in one, or several, classes of competition. Judged on its appearance and schooling as well as suitability for the class entered.

show jumping – jumping competitions.

stallion – male horse (not a gelding) more than three years old. Can be very difficult to control.

steeplechase – race run over fences on courses about 4 miles (7km) long. Name comes from old English tradition of racing between church steeples.

SPOTTER'S CHART

The horses and ponies on this chart are arranged in alphabetical order. When you see one, write down the date in the blank space next to each name. You might like to jot down the name of the place where you saw it, too, for a more complete record of your spotting.

Name of breed	Date	Name of breed	Date
Akhal-Teke		Connemara	
American Saddlebred		Criollo	
Andalusian		Dale	
Anglo-Arab		Dartmoor	
Appaloosa		Døle	
Arab (any type)		Don	
Ardennes		Dutch Draught	
Auxois		Exmoor	
Avelignese		Falabella	
Barb		Fell	
Boulonnais		Finnish	
Breton		Fjord	
Budyonny		Fredericksborg	
Camargue		Friesian	
Caspian		Gelderlander	
Cleveland Bay		Gotland	
Clydesdale		Groningen	

Name of breed	Date	Name of breed	Date
Hackney		Pinto	
Haflinger		Pinzgauer Noriker	
Hanoverian		Pony of the Americas	
Highland		Przewalski	
Holstein		Quarter Horse	
Huçul		Sable Island	
Icelandic		Schleswig	
Irish Draught		Shetland	
Jutland		Shire	
Karabair		Standardbred	
Kazakh		Suffolk Punch	
Kladruber		Tarpan	
Knabstrup		Tennessee Walking Horse	
Kustanair		Thoroughbred	
Lipizzaner		Trait du Nord	
Lusitano		Trakehner	
Morgan		Turkoman	
New Forest		Vladimir	
Nonius		Waler	
Oldenburger		Welsh Cob	
Orlov Trotter		Welsh Mountain	
Palomino		Wielkopolski	
Paso Fino			
Percheron			

INDEX

Akhal-Teke, 39
American Saddlebred, 33
Andalusian, 37, 44
Anglo-Arab, 32, 42
Appaloosa, 33
Arabs 6, 7, 8, 32, 36, 37, 40
Ardennes, 55
Auxois, 57
Avelignese, 58
Barb, 37, 45
Boulonnais, 59
Breton Heavy Draught, 56
Budyonny, 38
Camargue, 29
Caspian, 28
Cleveland Bay, 49
Clydesdale, 53
Connemara, 23
Criollo, 28
Dale, 21
Dartmoor, 22
Døle, 42
Don, 38
Draught horses 4, 7, 8, 53-59
Dutch Draught, 59
Exercising, 13
Exmoor, 6, 22
Falabella, 29
Feeding, 13, 14-15
Fell, 21
Finnish, 50
Fjord, 26
Frederiksborg, 51
Friesian, 47
Gelderlander, 47
Gotland, 25
Groningen, 48
Grooming, 16
Gudbrandsaal, see Døle
Hackney, 49
Haflinger, 25
Hanoverian, 43
Harness horses 4, 7, 46-52
Highland, 20
Holstein, 43
Hooves, 17
Huçul, 27
Icelandic, 26
Irish Draught, 54
Jutland, 58

Karabair, 39
Kazakh, 27
Kladruber, 51
Knabstrup, 44
Kustanair, 50
Lipizzaner, 44
Lusitano, 37
Markings, 9
Measuring height, 11
Morgan, 34
New Forest, 23
Nonius, 52
Oldenburger,48
Orlov Trotter,46
Palomino, 40
Paso Fino, 35
Percheron, 55
Pinto, 40
Pinzgauer Noriker, 56
Points of the horse, 10, 11
Polish Arab, 36
Ponies 20-31
Pony of the Americas, 31
Przewalski, 6, 30
Quarter Horse, 35
Riding horses, 32-45
Riding styles, 18
Russ, see Gotland
Sable Island Pony, 31
Schleswig, 59
Selle Français, 42
Shagya Arab, 36
Shetland, 20
Shire, 53
Shoeing, 17
Stabling, 13
Standardbred, 46
Suffolk Punch, 54
Tack (saddles and bridles), 19
Tarpan, 30
Tennessee Walking Horse, 34
Thoroughbred, 7, 8, 32
Trait du Nord, 57
Trakehner, 41
Turkoman, 41
Vladimir, 58
Waler, 45
Welsh Cob, 24
Welsh Mountain, 24
Wielkopolski, 52